Fun & Simple
Beads

Designed by Eddie Goldfine
Layout by Ariane Rybski
Edited by Shoshana Brickman
Photography by Danya Weiner

STERLING and the distinctive Sterling logo are registered trademarks of
Sterling Publishing Co., Inc.

Library of Congress Cataloging-in-Publication Data

Parnes, Tair, 1958–
Fun & simple beads / Tair Parnes ; photography by Danya Weiner.
    p. cm.
Includes index.
ISBN-13: 978-1-4027-3997-2
ISBN-10: 1-4027-3997-4
1. Beadwork. 2. Jewelry making. I. Title. II. Title: Fun and simple beads.
TT860.P375 2008
745.594'2—dc22   2007045253

2 4 6 8 10 9 7 5 3 1

Published by Sterling Publishing Co., Inc.
387 Park Avenue South, New York, NY 10016
© 2008 by Penn Publishing Ltd.
Distributed in Canada by Sterling Publishing
c/o Canadian Manda Group, 165 Dufferin Street,
Toronto, Ontario, Canada M6K 3H6
Distributed in the United Kingdom by GMC Distribution Services,
Castle Place, 166 High Street, Lewes, East Sussex, England BN7 1XU
Distributed in Australia by Capricorn Link (Australia) Pty. Ltd.
P.O. Box 704, Windsor, NSW 2756, Australia

Sterling ISBN-13: 978-1-4027-3997-2
ISBN-10: 1-4027-3997-4

For information about custom editions, special sales, premium and
corporate purchases, please contact Sterling Special Sales
Department at 800-805-5489 or specialsales@sterlingpublishing.com.

Fun & Simple

Beads

Tair Parnes

photography by DANYA WEINER

STERLING

New York / London
www.sterlingpublishing.com

Table of Contents

Introduction

D o you love beaded jewelry, but hesitate to try and make it yourself? Do you gaze at bead shops cautiously, as though there is some hidden secret to understanding how everything works? Do you wonder how to use all those sturdy strings, intricate clasps, and tiny tools to put beaded jewelry together?

Making beaded jewelry can seem overwhelming, but it's not. And, though you may feel as if you need a Ph.D. in Beading before trying to make a simple necklace or bracelet, you don't. Beads are incredibly manageable and user-friendly. The first step is no more complicated than poking a string through a hole.

Once you've got that mastered, and with a little help from the Basic Techniques (pages 12 and 13), you're ready to embark on the projects in this book. All you need are some basic tools (see Tools, pages 4 and 5) and a variety of diverse materials (see Materials, pages 6–11) and you'll be able to make a colorful range of necklaces, bracelets, earrings, rings, and brooches.

Your friends will be wowed when they see you wearing your handmade beaded masterpieces. Of course, there's no need to tell them how easy it was to make these projects. That's a secret you can keep to yourself!

So free your imagination, set your sights on some beautiful beads, and choose a project to start. You'll soon discover how beading can be simple and fun—and produce outstanding results.

About the Author

Tair Parnes is one of Tel Aviv's most exciting fashion designers. Inspired by diverse international influences, she excels at taking everyday items and turning them into unique objects of art. She is also an expert in making things as simple as possible. This means designing beautiful pieces of jewelry with ease, and explaining the process in simple terms. Tair has studied a wide range of art forms, from classic art and curatorship to weaving and working with gold. In addition to designing clothing, tapestries, and jewelry, Tair instructs people of all ages in the field of art appreciation, and teaches occupational therapy.

Tools & Materials

The first step in making any of these projects is making sure you have the supplies you need. The projects use a wide variety of beads, as well as materials such as fabric, construction paper, satin bows, and tassels. As for tools, you may need needles, pliers, scissors, or wire cutters. Don't be daunted by materials or tools you don't recognize! They can be found at beading shops, fabric stores, and general craft stores. The Internet is also an excellent source for finding supplies. It's a great way of shopping around for exactly what you want, and having it delivered to your door.

TOOLS

Needles come in various sizes. Be sure to choose a needle that is as thin as the hole in your smallest bead.

Beading needles

Beading needles have very small eyes and are perfect for stringing tiny seed beads. They are sized by number; the higher the number, the smaller the eye of the needle. For projects that include seed beads, choose a size 11 or 12 beading needle.

Embroidery needles are larger than beading needles and have relatively wide eyes. Use these needles when stringing beads onto embroidery floss, ribbon, or yarn.

Embroidery needles

Sewing needles are larger than beading needles but smaller than embroidery needles. Use them for sewing, and for stringing beads that have relatively large holes.

Flat-nose pliers

Pliers provide you with a set of tiny and precise fingers. A number of different types are available in most bead shops. The projects in this book make use of two types.

Flat-nose pliers have flat ends. They are excellent for opening and closing jump rings, and for holding jump rings steady while inserting them into beads. For instructions on how to open and close jump rings, see Basic Techniques (page 12).

Round-nose pliers

Round-nose pliers have round ends. They are perfect for making rounded loops in eye pins, head pins, and memory wire. They can also be used to open and close jump rings. For instructions on how to make rounded loops and how to open and close jump rings, see Basic Techniques (page 12).

These are the pliers referred to throughout the book, but **half round-flat pliers** (also known as **basic pliers**) are an excellent alternative.

Half round-flat pliers

Scissors are used to cut paper, thread, embroidery floss, paper, etc. Do not use scissors to cut wire, as this will wear down the blades.

Scissors

Nail scissors are handy for cutting circles with smooth edges, and for cutting fine thread.

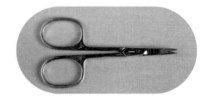

Nail scissors

Wire cutters are used to cut wire and trim head pins and eye pins. If you are using particularly thick wire, be sure to use sturdy cutters.

Wire cutters

Beading thread

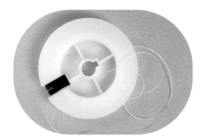

Beading thread

Elastic cord

Embroidery floss

MATERIALS

Chains come in an endless variety of styles, including cable, serpentine, rolo, and more. Don't be intimated by the names of the chains—just choose the shape you like best.

Construction paper is used to trace circles for making pom-poms. Any sturdy paper will do, so feel free to substitute with whatever you have on hand.

Stringing materials come in a wide variety of colors and widths. Choose the shade you like best, and don't compromise on quality—the sturdier the material you choose for stringing, the longer the life of your jewelry.

Beading thread is durable thread that doesn't tear or stretch. It is significantly stronger than sewing thread. Beading thread comes in various widths—be sure to select very thin thread when working with seed beads.

Elastic cord is great for making bracelets without clasps. It comes in a variety of widths; choose one that is thin enough to fit into your smallest bead.

Embroidery floss is multi-strand thread used for embroidery, crochet, hair wraps, and other crafts. It comes in an endless variety of colors, and can be found in sewing stores and craft stores.

Memory wire

Memory wire is flexible wire that retains its shape and conforms to a certain size after it has been worn a few times. It comes in sizes suitable for bracelets, necklaces, and rings.

Waxed cotton cord

Waxed cotton cord comes in various colors and widths. Make sure the cord you choose is thin enough to fit through the holes in your smallest beads.

Beads are available in a vast array of colors, sizes, and materials. They also come in countless shapes, including squares, tubes, hearts, stars, and leaves. The beads described below are used in the projects in this book, but don't hesitate to substitute.

Crystal beads

Crystal beads are elegant beads made from glass or crystal. They come in a variety of shapes, including drops, balls, cubes, and cones.

Fabric beads

Fabric beads have a texture and appearance that is singularly distinct. They can be found in select bead shops and on the Internet.

Glass beads come in vibrant colors, diverse shapes, and a wide range of sizes. They also come in a range of prices, so select beads that fit your budget. Glass beads are often sold in assorted packages, giving you a maximum selection of styles.

Glass beads

Knitted beads have a soft knitted surface, bringing a gentle touch to your jewelry. They can be found at bead shops and on the Internet.

Knitted beads

Beads (continued)

Metal beads may be made from various materials, including sterling silver, gold, and pewter. They come in diverse shapes and sizes, including flowers, leaves, and hearts.

Metal beads

Natural seed beads are made from the seeds of real plants. Bibakao and Bodhi seeds are natural seeds often used for beaded work.

Plastic beads are lightweight and inexpensive. They often have particularly large holes, so stringing them is easy. You can find plastic beads at bead shops and craft stores, as well as many toy stores.

Natural seed beads

Seed beads are small round beads that come in a wide variety of sizes, colors, and finishes. They are sized by aught (°) rather than inches or millimeters; the higher the number, the smaller the bead. The projects in this book use sizes 11°, 8°, and 6° seed beads.

Shell beads and buttons are made from natural shells such as paua and cowrie. They come in various shapes and sizes.

Shell beads and buttons

Fabric glue is used to stick satin bows together. It can be found in fabric stores and craft stores.

Jewelry findings are the metal items that finish off a piece of jewelry. They may be made from a range of materials, including

sterling silver, gold, and pewter. Always choose high-quality findings, as you don't want them to rust or break.

Bead caps are small pieces of metal that cradle beads, adding a finished, decorated touch. Select the size of your bead caps according to your beads, as you want them to fit snugly.

Charm ring bases are usually made from sterling silver or stainless steel. They come with a hole for attaching charms, and are available in various sizes.

Clasps are those things we fiddle with when putting on and taking off necklaces and bracelets. Some clasps close with a jump ring or loop, others have two hooks. I generally use two-part clasps made from a lobster claw and jump ring, but you can choose any clasp that complements your design (and is easy to open and close).

Connector bars have a single loop on one side and several loops on the other. They support strings of beads and clasps.

Crimp beads are small tubes with thin walls that are easily flattened. Crimped onto your stringing material, they hold beads or clasps in place.

Drops have one or several loops, and provide a base for making earrings or pendants. Filigree drops include delicate decoration made with twisted gold or silver threads.

Bead caps

Clasps

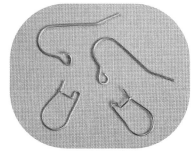

Ear wires

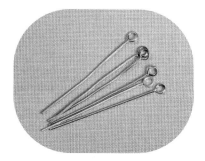

Eye pins

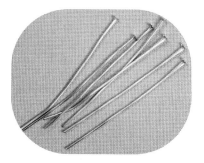

Head pins

Jump rings

Jewelry findings (continued)

Ear wires turn beaded masterpieces into dangling earrings. Small hoop earrings can also be used as a base for earrings.

Eye pins are straight pins with a loop at one end. The loop stops beads from falling off and provides a site for connecting the beads to other objects. Eye pins come in various lengths and widths.

Head pins are straight pins with a flat base at one end to keep beads from falling off. Head pins come in various lengths and widths.

Jump rings are small connector rings. When purchasing rings for the projects in this book, be sure to select open jump rings rather than ones that have been soldered shut.

Kilt pins look like the pins traditionally used to hold together plaid skirts. Loops at the bottom allow you to attach ornaments and decorations.

Pin backs are used for making brooches.

Satin bows are used in several projects to add a colorful, whimsical touch. They can be purchased in a wide range of colors and sizes at fabric stores and craft stores. For instructions on how to make bows yourself, see Basic Techniques (page 12).

Satin fabric is light and shiny. It may be made of silk, nylon, or polyester, and can be purchased in fabric stores and craft stores.

Super glue is used to reinforce knots. It is sold in many bead shops as well as craft stores and hardware stores. Be sure to choose glue that is quick-drying and water-resistant, and has a fine spout for precise application.

Tassels are made from strands of chain or string. They can be found in bead shops, fabric stores, and craft stores.

Basic Techniques

Opening and closing jump rings

The easiest way to open and close jump rings is to use two sets of pliers. Two flat-nose pliers are best, but you can also use round-nose pliers. If you have only one set of pliers, that's fine too; you'll just have to grasp one end of the jump ring with your fingers.

To open the jump ring, hold one set of pliers in each hand and grasp one end of the jump ring in each set of pliers. Position the jump ring so that the hole is facing you, then draw one pair of pliers toward you and push the other pair away. ***Do not unroll the jump ring.*** To close the ring, draw the pliers back to their original position.

Making loops in head pins and eye pins

To make loops that are tidy and secure, string your beads onto the pin and draw down to the flat or looped end. Using round-nose pliers, grasp the wire just above the topmost bead and bend into a single or double loop, whichever you prefer. Use wire cutters to cut any excess wire.

Tying a picture-perfect bow

Decorative satin bows are easy to purchase, but if you'd like to make them yourself, simply follow these steps. To make a bow that is about 1½" (4 cm) long, start with a piece of satin ribbon measuring about 10" (25 cm). (It's easier to work with a longer piece of ribbon, then trim any extra when you're finished.) Form the ends of the ribbon into two equal loops, leaving small tails on each loop. Cross the right loop over the left loop and make sure there is a small hole at the bottom. Wrap the right loop over the left loop and draw it through the hole. Pull the loops and tails gently to secure the knot. Adjust the loops so they are even and trim the tails if they are too long.

Necklaces

Satin Surprise Necklace

Don't tell anyone the secret behind making these silky beads, and they'll never guess how simple it was!

MATERIALS

3 yards (2.75 m) of satin fabric, various shades of green and blue

30 plastic beads, ½" to 1¼" (1.3 cm to 3 cm) in diameter, various shapes and colors

Beading thread, blue or green

TOOLS

Scissors

Sewing needle

1. Cut the satin into 30 circles, ranging in size from 2¾" (7 cm) to 4" (10 cm) in diameter. You can trace the bottom of a cup or coaster for the circles, or draw them freehand. You'll be using the satin to wrap the beads—and you want at least ½" (1.3 cm) of extra satin all around for bunching at the top—so make sure the circles are big enough for your beads (Figure A).

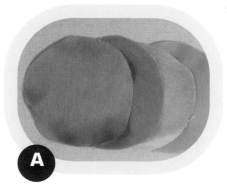

2. Thread the needle with a comfortable length of thread, fold the thread in half, and tie the ends together.

3. Place a bead in the middle of a satin circle so that the hole of the bead is flat on your work surface and in the center of the satin (Figure B).

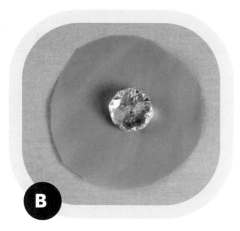

B

C

4. Wrap the bead by gathering the edges of the satin into a bunch at the top. Take care that the bead doesn't roll as you wrap it and that the hole stays directly below the gathered satin.

5. Wrap the thread around the satin at the top of the bead and tie in a double knot. Sew a few stitches to secure the bead in place, tie a knot, and cut the thread close to the knot (Figure C).

6. Repeat Steps 3 to 5 to wrap all of the beads. You may want to trim the satin at the top if some beads are particularly small (Figure D).

7. Thread the needle with a 70" (180 cm) piece of thread, fold the thread in half, and tie the ends together, leaving a 3" (7.6 cm) tail.

TIP

The beads are covered in this project, so you can use any beads you have on hand—even plastic children's beads. Also, because the beads are quite large, there's no need to fuss with a thin-eyed beading needle.

8. String the wrapped beads onto the thread, making sure all of the beads are oriented in the same direction. Draw the beads close together, so that the bunched end of one bead is flush against the smooth end of the adjacent bead (Figure E).

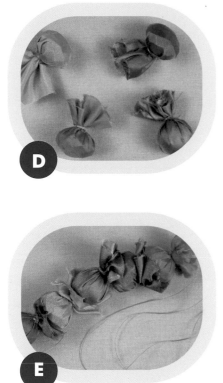

D

E

9. When all of the beads have been strung, tie the ends of the necklace together with a secure double knot and cut the thread close to the knot.

Shimmering Shell Necklace

You'll draw the pearls out of their shells with this aquamarine necklace.

MATERIALS

250–300 seed beads, sizes 6°, 8°, 11°, various shades of green and blue

2 turquoise glass beads, ¼" (0.6 cm) in diameter

2 green glass beads, ¼" (0.6 cm) in diameter

2 light blue glass beads, ¼" (0.6 cm) in diameter

Round shell pendant, 2" (5 cm) in diameter, with 1 hole at the top and 5 holes at the bottom

Beading thread

Super glue

Two-part silver clasp

TOOLS

Scissors

Beading needle

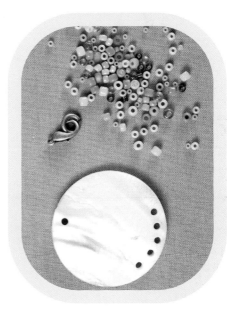

1. Thread the needle with a comfortable length of thread, fold the thread in half, and tie the ends together, leaving a 2" (5 cm) tail.

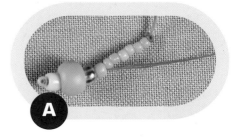

2. String 6 size 11° beads, 1 size 8° bead, 1 size 6° bead, 1 turquoise glass bead, 1 size 6° bead, and 1 size 11° bead. Loop the thread around the last bead and draw it back through the previous 4 beads (Figure A).

3. String 6 size 11° beads (Figure B).

4. Insert the thread into the leftmost hole at the bottom of the pendant. Tie a double knot in the thread and secure with a dab of super glue. Cut the thread close to the knot (Figure C).

5. Tie the ends of the remaining thread together, leaving a 2" (5 cm) tail. String 6 size 11° beads, 1 size 8° bead, 1 size 6° bead, 1 green glass bead, 1 size 6° bead, 1 size 8° bead, and 1 size 11° bead. Loop the thread around the last bead and draw it back through the previous 5 beads. String 6 size 11° beads (Figure D).

6. Insert the thread into the adjacent hole on the pendant. Tie a double knot in the thread and secure with a dab of super glue. Cut the thread close to the knot (Figure E).

7. Tie the ends of the remaining thread together, leaving a 2" (5 cm) tail. String 6 size 11° beads, 2 size 8° beads, 1 size 6° bead, 2 light blue glass beads, 1 size 6° bead, and 1 size 11° bead. Loop the thread around

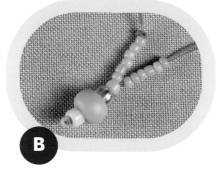

B

C

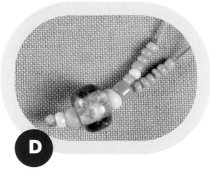

D

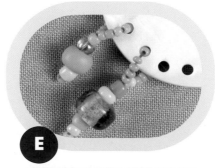

E

the last bead and draw it back through the previous 6 beads. String 6 size 11° beads (Figure F).

8. Insert the thread into the center hole at the bottom of the pendant. Tie a double knot in the thread and secure with a dab of super glue. Cut the thread close to the knot (Figure G).

9. Tie the ends of the remaining thread together, leaving a 2" (5 cm) tail. Repeat Steps 2 to 3 and Step 5 to make 2 more fringes (Figure H).

10. Attach these fringes to the empty holes at the bottom of the pendant so that the pendant is symmetrical (Figure I).

11. Thread the needle with a 40" (101 cm) piece of thread, fold it in half, and tie the ends together. Tie one half of the clasp at one end of the thread and begin stringing seed beads, alternating colors and sizes (Figure J)

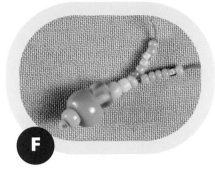

F

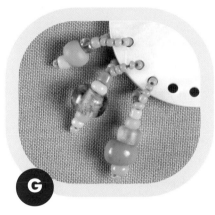

G

H

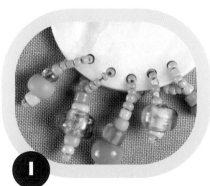

I

J

K

L

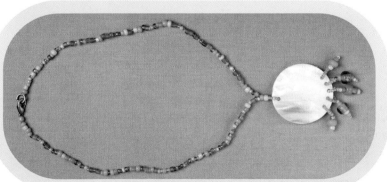

12. Continue stringing beads until the necklace is half the desired length. Measure against your neck as you work to find the right length for you.

13. String 10 size 11° beads, then draw the thread through the single hole at the top of the pendant. Draw the thread back through the last 3 beads, then continue stringing beads, alternating colors and sizes (Figure K).

14. When both halves of the necklace are even, tie the other half of the clasp to the necklace. Pull the thread taut as you tie on the clasp, so that it is flush against the beads. Secure with a dab of super glue and cut the thread close to the knot (Figure L).

23

Tempting Tassel Necklace

Show off some super special beads with this playful piece.

MATERIALS

1 large glass bead, 1¼" (3 cm) in length

1 flat flower bead, ¾" (1.9 cm) in diameter

4 medium glass beads, various colors and styles

1 silver leaf bead, 1" (2.5 cm) in length

2 seed beads, green

1 silver chain tassel

1 talon pendant

5 pairs of silver bead caps, sized to fit the large glass beads

4 silver eye pins

2 silver head pins

7 silver jump rings, ¼" (0.6 cm) in diameter

2½" (6.3 cm) piece of thin silver chain

24" (61 cm) piece of waxed cotton cord, green

2 silver crimp beads, sized to fit the cotton cord

Silver clasp

TOOLS

Scissors

Round-nose pliers

Wire cutters

2 flat-nose pliers

1. String a pair of bead caps and the large glass bead onto an eye pin so that the bead caps cradle the bead. Make a loop in the eye pin and trim any excess wire (Figure A).

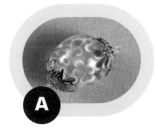

A

2. String a pair of bead caps and the flower bead onto an eye pin so that the bead caps cradle the bead. Make a loop in the eye pin and trim any excess wire (Figure B).

3. String a pair of bead caps and a glass bead onto a head pin so that the bead caps cradle the bead. Make a loop in the head pin and trim any excess wire. Attach a jump ring to the loop (Figure C).

4. String a pair of bead caps and a glass bead onto an eye pin so that the bead caps cradle the bead. Make a loop in the eye pin and trim any excess wire. String the leaf bead onto one of the loops. Cut a 1" (2.5 cm) piece of chain and string onto the other loop. Attach a jump ring to the chain (Figure D).

5. String a seed bead, a glass bead, and another seed bead onto a head pin. Make a loop in the head pin and trim any excess wire. String the remaining 1½" (3.8 cm) piece of chain onto the loop and attach a jump ring to the chain (Figure E).

B

C

D

E

F

G

TIP
Beads caps are perfect for framing round beads when stringing them onto head pins and eye pins. For heart beads, flower beads, or star beads, try using seed beads to frame the beads instead.

6. String a pair of bead caps and a glass bead onto an eye pin so that the bead caps cradle the bead. Make a loop in the eye pin and trim any excess wire. Attach the tassel to one of the loops and attach a jump ring to the other loop (Figure F).

7. To make the pendant, attach the large bead from Step 1 to the flower bead from Step 2. Attach a jump ring to the empty loop on the flower bead. Attach the talon and the beads from Steps 3 to 6 to the jump ring (Figure G).

8. String the cord through the top loop of the pendant and draw the pendant along until it lies in the middle of the cord. Tie a knot just above the pendant to secure in place.

9. String a crimp bead onto one end of the cord and draw along the cord for about 1" (2.5 cm). String a jump ring onto the cord. Loop the end of the cord over the jump ring and draw it into the crimp bead. Use the flat-nose pliers to flatten the crimp bead over the end of the cord and trim any excess cord.

10. Repeat Step 9 at the other end of the cord. Attach the clasp to one end of the necklace (Figure H).

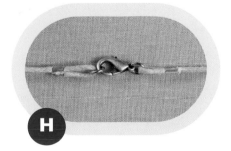

H

Pom-Pom Necklace

This necklace uses of a cornucopia of materials, including fabric beads, knitted beads, and handmade pom-poms. Fun and funky, it's definitely something to cheer about.

MATERIALS

Construction paper

Embroidery floss, various shades of green and pink

55" (140 cm) piece of pink organza ribbon

4 fabric beads, various shades of green and pink, 1" (2.5 cm) in diameter

16 knitted beads, various shades of green and pink, ¾" (1.9 cm) in diameter

4 glass beads, ¾" (1.9 cm) in length

TOOLS

Pencil

Scissors

Large-eyed embroidery needle

1. To make the pom-poms, draw 18 circles, each with a diameter of about 1½" (3.8 cm), onto the construction paper. You can trace the bottom of a cup or coaster for the circles, or draw them freehand. Cut a ½" (1.3 cm) hole in the center of each circle (Figure A).

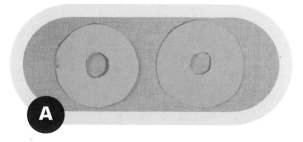

A

2. Thread the needle with a comfortable length of embroidery floss, fold the floss in half, and tie the ends together.

3. Hold 2 circles together so that the holes are lined up. Wrap the circles with floss by drawing the floss up through the hole, wrapping it around the outside of the circles, and drawing it back up through the hole. Continue wrapping until the hole is full of floss (Figures B and C).

4. Cut the floss along the edge of the circles, taking care to cut each piece (Figure D).

5. Cut a comfortable length of floss and slip it between the cardboard circles. Draw it around the middle of the circles and tie in a double knot. Make sure the knot is very secure, as this is what holds the pom-pom together (Figure E).

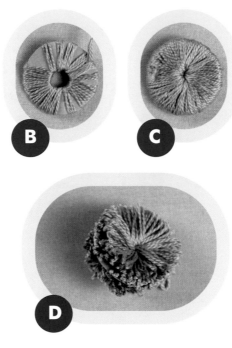

B

C

D

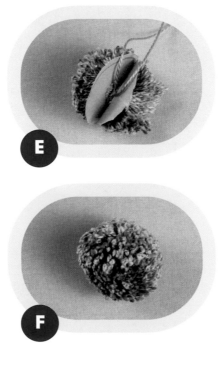

E

F

6. Cut the cardboard circles to remove them from the pom-pom. Roll the pom-pom between your hands to fluff it out evenly (Figure F).

7. Repeat Steps 2 to 6, using various colors of floss, to make a total of 9 pom-poms.

8. Thread the needle with the ribbon. String a fabric bead, a pom-pom, and a fabric bead onto the ribbon and draw them along until they are about 8" (20 cm) from the other end (Figure G).

9. Continue stringing groups of beads and pom-poms onto the ribbon until you are about 8" (20 cm) from the other end. To finish, tie the ends of the ribbon in a bow.

Sally Sells Seashells Necklace

There's no better way of celebrating summer than by adorning yourself with seashells. Luckily, the shells in this necklace can be found in most bead stores—perfect for landlubbing city-dwellers.

MATERIALS

250 seed beads, sizes 6°, 8°, 11°, various colors

25 cowrie shell beads

Beading thread

Super glue

TOOLS

Scissors

Beading needle

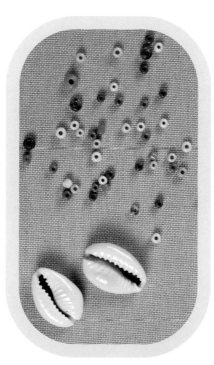

1. Thread the needle with a 40" (101 cm) piece of thread, fold the thread in half, and tie the ends together.

TIP
This design also looks great as a choker or anklet. Measure as you go along and end with a shell when you reach the right length.

2. String 22 seed beads, alternating colors and sizes. Make a loop by drawing the thread through the first bead, then string 7 more beads. This loop forms half of the clasp. The other half is a shell, so set aside one that fits snugly into the loop (Figure A).

B

A

C

D

3. String a shell bead onto the thread, then draw your thread back through the last bead. String 11 more beads, alternating colors and sizes (Figure B).

4. Repeat Step 3 until your necklace is the right length.

5. To finish, string the shell bead you set aside in Step 2 onto the thread. Draw the thread back through the last bead and tie in a double knot. Add a dab of super glue to secure and cut the thread close to the knot (Figures C and D).

Eclectic Eye-Catcher Necklace

This composition of colorful beads and thick chains is certain to attract an abundance of admiring glances.

MATERIALS

50 seed beads, various sizes and colors

25 large beads, ½" to 1" (1.3 to 2.5 cm) in diameter, various colors and styles

6 red satin bows

25 silver head pins

33 silver jump rings, ¼" (0.6 cm) in diameter

Fabric glue

71" (183 cm) piece of thick silver chain

Silver clasp

TOOLS

Round-nose pliers

Wire cutters

2 flat-nose pliers

1. String a seed bead and a large bead onto a head pin. Make a loop in the head pin and trim any excess wire. Attach a jump ring to the loop. Repeat to string all of the large beads onto head pins (Figure A).

2. Attach a jump ring to each satin bow. Add a dab of fabric glue to secure the jump ring in place (Figure B).

3. Cut the chain into 3 pieces, in the following lengths: 46" (117 cm), 15" (38 cm), and 10" (25 cm).

D

4. Working with the longest chain first, measure 13" (33 cm) from one end and attach one of the beads from Step 1 (Figure C).

5. Measure about 1½" (3.8 cm) from this bead and attach another bead. Repeat 10 times (Figure D).

6. Attach 9 beads to the 15" (38 cm) chain and 5 beads to the 10" (25 cm) chain in a similar manner, taking care that the beads are evenly spaced.

B

E

7. Attach the shorter chains to the longer chain at the points where the first and last beads are attached (Figure E).

8. Attach the bows to beads in a random fashion.

C

F

9. To finish, attach the clasp to one end of the necklace (Figure F).

Earth, Wind, and Fire Necklace

This striking design features earthy browns, breezy blues, and fiery reds.

MATERIALS

30 natural seed beads, red and brown

4 red heart beads, ¾" (1.9 cm) in length

4 flat green glass beads, ¾" (1.9 cm) in diameter

8 round glass beads, ¾" (1.9 cm) in diameter, various shades of green and blue

8 cowrie shell beads

47" (119 cm) piece of waxed cotton cord, green

Three 47" (119 cm) pieces of waxed cotton cord, brown

TOOLS

Scissors

1. This necklace is made up of 2 similar and separate strands, so divide the beads into 2 groups and set one group aside.

2. Tie together the green cord and a brown cord, leaving a 2" (5 cm) tail.

3. String a red seed bead onto each cord and tie the cords together (Figures A and B).

4. String a heart bead onto the brown cord and tie the cords together (Figures C and D).

C

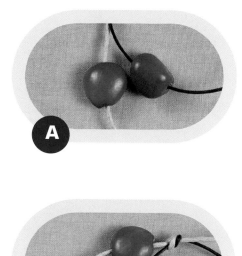

A

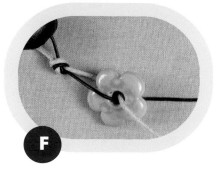

D

5. String a red seed bead onto the brown cord and tie the cords together. String a brown seed bead onto the brown cord and tie the cords together (Figure E).

6. String a flat glass bead by drawing the green cord under the bead and out through the top, and draw the brown cord over the bead and out through the bottom (Figure F). Tie the cords together.

7. String a round glass bead onto the green cord and tie the cords together.

8. String a shell bead onto a cord and tie a knot in the cord. String a shell bead onto the other cord and tie a knot in the cord (Figure G).

B

E

F

G

9. Continue stringing beads in this manner until the necklace is the right length, then tie all 4 ends together (Figure H).

H

10. String the rest of the beads onto the remaining brown cords to make a second necklace that is similar, although not necessarily identical.

Pink Flower Power Necklace

For a flower that never wilts, try this playful design. Increase the number of flowers in your necklace to make up a whole bouquet!

MATERIALS

6 red seed beads, size 6°

26 pink seed beads, size 8°

80–100 glass beads, various colors and shapes

Beading thread

Two-part silver clasp

Super glue

TOOLS

Scissors

Beading needle

1. Thread the needle with a comfortable length of thread, fold the thread in half, and tie the ends together.

2. String the red beads onto the thread. Take care that they don't fall off, as they have relatively large holes.

3. Draw the thread together on either end of the beads to form a ring of beads and tie in a double knot (Figure A).

4. String 6 pink beads, then draw the thread through a red bead to make a petal of pink beads. Draw the thread through an adjacent red bead (Figure B).

A

B

C

D

E

F

5. String 5 pink beads, then draw the thread through the closest and bottommost pink bead in the adjacent petal. Draw the thread through a red bead to make another petal, then draw the thread through an adjacent red bead (Figure C).

6. Repeat Step 5 until the flower is complete, then tie the thread in a double knot and secure with a dab of super glue. Cut the thread close to the knot (Figure D).

7. Thread the needle with a 60" (152 cm) piece of thread, fold the thread in half, and tie the ends together.

8. String half of the clasp onto the thread and secure with a double knot. Begin stringing glass beads (Figure E).

9. Continue stringing beads onto the thread, measuring against your neck as you go. When you reach the halfway mark, draw the thread through 3 beads at the top of one of the petals in the flower (Figure F).

10. String the rest of the glass beads onto the thread until both sides of the necklace are even.

11. String on the other half of the clasp and secure with a double knot. Add a dab of super glue and cut the thread close to the knot (Figure G).

G

Bracelets

Bonfire on the Beach Bracelet

This collection of fiery red and sandy brown beads conjures memories of summer bonfires. Incorporating cowrie shell beads adds a bit of the beach.

MATERIALS

8 natural seed beads, yellow and red, ½" to ¾" (1 cm to 1.9 cm) in diameter

3 round glass beads, red and orange, ¼" (0.6 cm) in diameter

4 cowrie shell beads

1 red heart bead, ¾" (1.9 cm) in length

Two 23" (58.4 cm) pieces of waxed cotton cord, brown

Two-part silver clasp

Super glue

TOOLS

Scissors

2 flat-nosed pliers

1. String both cords onto the clasp and draw them through until you reach the halfway mark. Fold the cords in half so you have 4 even strands and tie them in a knot close to the clasp (Figure A).

A

2. Divide the strands into 2 pairs and tie a knot in each pair. String a red seed bead onto a pair of strands and tie a knot. String a red seed bead onto the other pair and tie a knot (Figure B).

3. String a glass bead onto a strand and tie the pair in a knot. String a yellow seed bead onto a strand in the other pair of strands and tie the pair in a knot (Figure C).

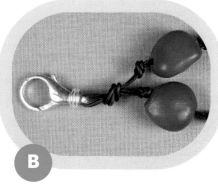

4. String a shell bead onto a strand and tie the pair in a knot. String a glass bead onto a strand in the other pair and tie the pair in a knot (Figure D).

5. Continue stringing beads in this manner, measuring against your wrist as you go and making sure both strands are even.

6. When the bracelet is the right length, draw all of the strands into the other half of the clasp and tie in a secure knot. Reinforce with a dab of super glue and cut the cords close to the knot (Figure E).

Tickled Pink Bracelet

Feminine and funky, the bold beads and delicate bows in this piece will tickle the fancy of anyone who fancies pink.

MATERIALS

25–30 large glass beads, various shapes and shades of pink

5 pink satin bows

25–30 silver eye pins

19 silver jump rings, ¼" (0.6 cm) in diameter

2 silver 6-strand connector bars

Fabric glue

Two-part silver clasp

TOOLS

Wire cutters

Round-nose pliers

2 flat-nose pliers

1. String a bead onto an eye pin. Make a loop and trim any excess wire. Repeat to string all of the beads onto eye pins (Figure A).

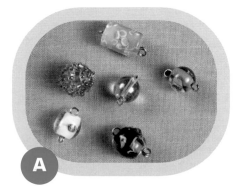

A

2. Attach a jump ring to each satin bow. Add a dab of fabric glue to secure the jump ring in place (Figure B).

3. Attach jump rings to the 6 loops on one of the connector bars (Figure C).

4. String a bead onto 2 adjacent jump rings on the connector bar. Repeat to attach 3 beads to the 6 jump rings (Figure D).

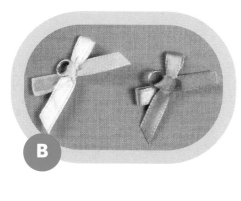

B

C

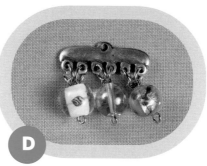

D

E

F

5. Attach a bead to each of the beads you attached in Step 4 (Figure E).

6. Continue connecting beads in this manner until the bracelet is the right length. The beads are different sizes, so make sure that all 3 chains are the same length.

7. Attach 2 jump rings onto the last bead in each chain. Attach each jump ring to one of the 6 loops on the other connector bar.

8. Attach the bows to the chains in a random fashion.

9. To finish, attach jump rings to the single loop on each of the connector bars and attach the clasp (Figure F).

Candy Shop Bracelet

What could be sweeter than candy on a stick?
A ring of candy around your wrist, of course!

MATERIALS

80–100 glass beads, various shapes, sizes, and colors

14–18 silver head pins, ¾" (1.9 cm) in length

Elastic cord

Super glue

TOOLS

Round-nose pliers

Wire cutters

Scissors

1. String 2 to 4 beads onto a head pin. Make a loop in the head pin and trim any excess wire.

2. Repeat Step 1 to decorate all of the head pins. Each head pin should be different, but all of them should be about ½" (1.3 cm) long, so adjust the number of beads accordingly (Figure A).

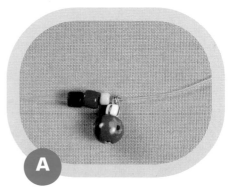

3. Cut a piece of cord that is 4" (10 cm) longer than the length of the bracelet you want to make. Tie a knot at one end, leaving a 2½" (6.3 cm) tail.

4. String 3 glass beads and 1 decorated head pin onto the cord (Figure B).

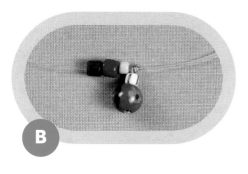

TIP

You can also use regular beading thread to make this bracelet, just be sure to add a clasp.

5. Repeat Step 4 until the bracelet is the right length (Figure C).

6. To finish, tie the ends of the bracelet together with a secure double knot. Reinforce with a dab of super glue and cut the ends close to the knot.

Charming Charm Bracelet

Mix and match beads and techniques for variety.

MATERIALS

11 turquoise seed beads, size 6°

11 large beads, glass, plastic or stone, various sizes and shades of turquoise

3 cowrie shell beads

1 silver leaf pendant, ¾" (1.9 cm) in length

1 heart outline pendant

50 turquoise seed beads, size 11°

1 tube bead, ¼" (0.6 cm) in length

6 small heart pendants, ¼" (0.6 cm) in length

11 head pins

3 eye pins

24 silver jump rings, ¼" (0.6 cm) in diameter

5 pairs of silver bead caps, sized to fit the large beads

Beading thread

Two 8" (20 cm) pieces of thick silver chain

Silver clasp

TOOLS

Round-nose pliers

Wire cutters

2 flat-nose pliers

Scissors

Beading needle

1. To make a dangling charm, string a size 6° seed bead onto a head pin. Make a loop in the head pin and trim any excess wire. Repeat to make 6 decorated head pins.

2. String a large bead onto an eye pin. Make a loop in the eye pin and trim any excess wire. Attach the beads from Step 1 to one of the loops and attach a jump ring to the other loop (Figure A).

3. To make a heart charm, attach a jump ring to the heart outline pendant. Attach a second jump ring to the first jump ring (Figure B).

4. To make a simple bead charm, string a size 6° seed bead and one of the large beads onto a head pin. Make a loop in the head pin and trim any excess wire. Attach a jump ring to the loop. Repeat to make 5 simple bead charms (Figure C).

5. To make a cradled bead charm, string a pair of bead caps and a large bead onto a head pin so that the bead caps cradle the bead. Make a loop in

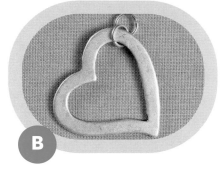

B

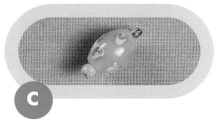

C

D

E

A

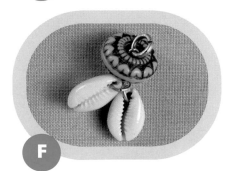

F

the head pin and trim any excess wire. Attach a jump ring to the loop. Repeat to make 4 cradled bead charms (Figure D).

6. Attach the leaf pendant to one of the simple bead charms from Step 5 and attach another jump ring.

7. Attach jump rings to each of the shell beads.

8. To make a simple shell charm, attach a second jump ring to one of the shell beads (Figure E).

9. To make a dangling shell charm, string a large bead onto an eye pin. Make a loop in the eye pin and trim any excess wire. Attach the 2 remaining shell beads from Step 7 to one of the loops. Attach a jump ring to the other loop (Figure F).

10. To make a beaded tassel charm, thread the needle with a comfortable length of thread. Fold the thread in half, tie the ends together, and tie to the loop of an eye pin.

11. String 10 size 11° seed beads onto the thread. Loop the thread around the last bead and draw it back through the previous 9 beads. Draw the thread through the loop in the eye pin and secure with a knot.

12. Repeat Step 11 to make 5 strands of beads extending from the eye pin (Figure G).

13. String the tube bead onto the eye pin. Make a loop in the eye pin and trim any excess wire. Attach a jump ring to the loop (Figure H).

14. To make a dangling heart charm, string the small heart pendants onto a jump ring. Attach a second jump ring to the first jump ring (Figure I).

15. Attach 8 charms to one of the chains (Figure J).

16. Attach the remaining charms to the other chain and connect the ends of the chains together with jump rings. To finish, attach a clasp to one end of the bracelet and a jump ring to the other end (Figure K).

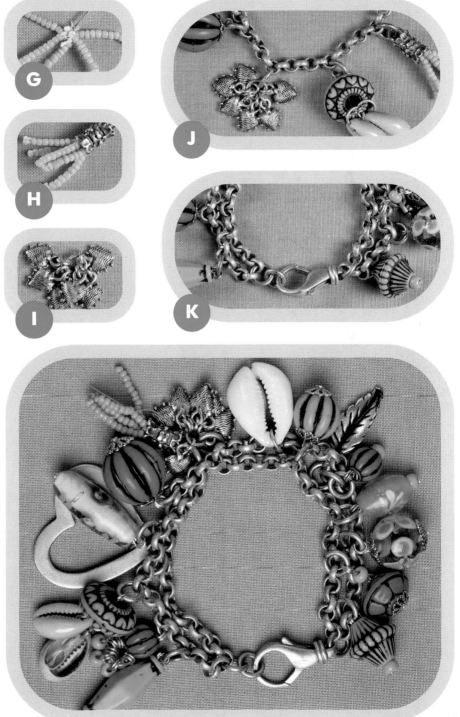

Earrings

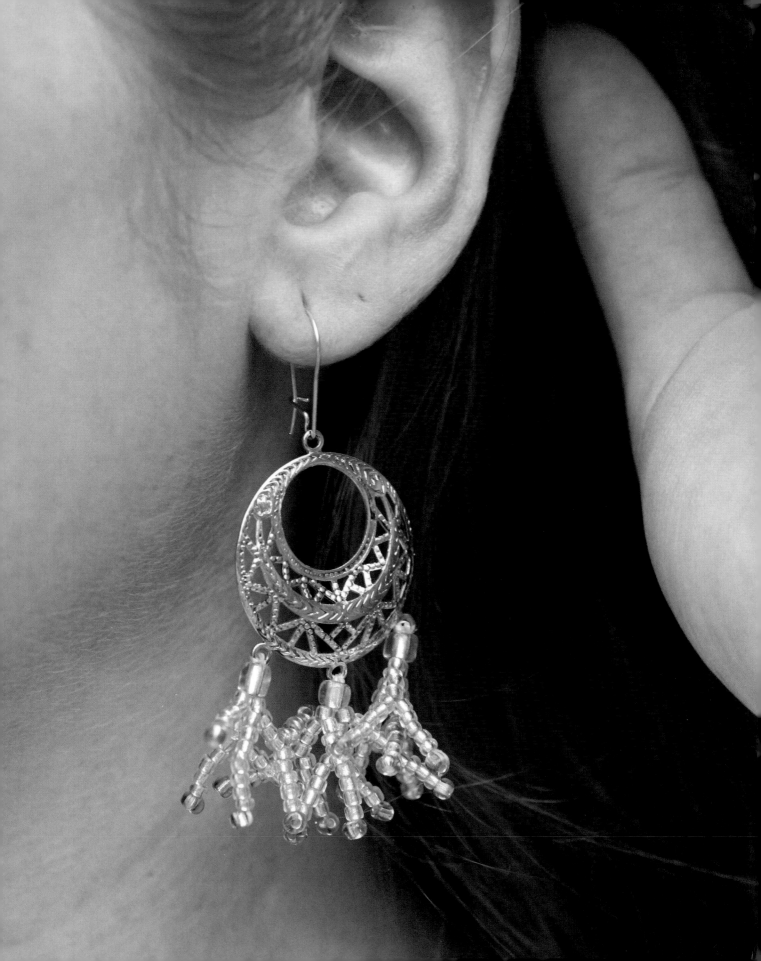

Fringed Fairy Earrings

With pastel pink beads and delicate gold filigrees, these earrings are perfect for fairies, princesses, and every other dainty creature.

MATERIALS

6 pink seed beads, size 6°

138 pink seed beads, size 11°

36 gold seed beads, size 8°

Pair of gold 3-loop filigree drops

Pair of gold ear wires

Beading thread

TOOLS

Beading needle

Scissors

1. Thread the needle with a comfortable length of thread, fold the thread in half, and tie the ends together.

2. Tie the thread to a loop in one of the filigree drops and string a size 6° pink bead.

3. String 9 size 11° pink beads and a gold bead. Loop the thread around the gold bead and draw it back through 5 pink beads.

4. String 5 size 11° pink beads and a gold bead. Loop the thread around the gold bead and draw it back through 5 pink beads. Now draw the thread through 2 beads in the main stem of the fringe.

5. String 9 size 11° pink beads and a gold bead. Loop the thread around the gold bead and draw it back through 9 pink beads. Now draw the thread up the main stem of the fringe and through the size 6° pink bead at the top.

6. Draw the thread through the loop in the filigree and out through the same size 6° pink bead.

7. Repeat Steps 3 to 5 to make another fringe dangling from this loop, then draw the thread through the loop and tie in a secure double knot. Cut the thread close to the knot (Figure A).

A

B

C

8. Tie the thread to the adjacent loop in the filigree drop and string a size 6° pink bead. Repeat Steps 3 to 7 to make fringes from the loop (Figure B).

9. Tie the thread to the last loop in the filigree drop, string a size 6° pink bead, and repeat Steps 3 to 7 (Figure C).

10. Repeat Steps 1 to 9 to make the second earring. To finish, attach each earring to an ear wire.

Double Rainbow Chip Earrings

These earrings look as delicious as a double scoop of ice cream.

MATERIALS

116–136 seed beads, various sizes and colors

12 flat round shell beads, ¼" (0.6 cm) in diameter

12 silver head pins

Memory wire for rings

4 silver jump rings, ⅛" (0.3 cm) in diameter

2 silver jump rings, ¼" (0.6 cm) in diameter

Pair of silver ear wires

TOOLS

Round-nose pliers

2 flat-nose pliers

Wire cutters

TIP

You may need to play around with the number and size of beads in each section of the coils to make each earring symmetrical.

1. String a seed bead, a shell bead, and a seed bead onto a head pin. Make a loop in the head pin and trim any excess wire. Repeat to make 6 decorated head pins (Figure A).

2. Cut 2 coils of memory wire and make a loop at one end of each coil with the round-nose pliers (Figure B).

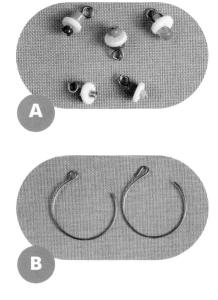

A

B

3. String 7–9 seed beads, alternating sizes and colors, onto one of the coils.

4. String a decorated head pin from Step 1, then string 2 seed beads. String another decorated head pin, then string 2 more seed beads. Repeat to string 5 decorated head pins in this manner, ending with a head pin.

5. String 7–9 seed beads, alternating sizes and colors. Make sure the head pins hang in the middle of the coil, then make a loop after the last bead (Figure C).

6. Insert small jump rings onto the loops at either end of the coil.

7. Working now with the other coil, string 8–10 seed beads, alternating sizes and colors. String one of the jump rings from Step 6.

8. String 8–10 seed beads, alternating sizes and colors, then string the other jump ring from Step 6.

9. String 8–10 seed beads, alternating sizes and colors,

onto the other end of the coil. Make sure the first coil hangs in the middle of the second coil, then make a loop after the last bead (Figure D).

10. Open a large jump ring and string onto one of the loops in the top coil. String the remaining decorated head pin, string the other loop in the top coil, then close the jump ring (Figure E).

11. Repeat Steps 1 to 10 to make the second earring. To finish, attach each earring to an ear wire.

Little Bow Peep Earrings

If nursery rhyme characters could talk, we know one in particular that would favor these pretty earrings.

MATERIALS

2 pink satin bows

2 heart beads, ½" to ¾" (1.3 cm to 1.9 cm) in length

48 seed beads, sizes 6° and 8°, various shades of pink

4 silver jump rings, ¼" (0.6 cm) in diameter

50 head pins

Two 8" (20 cm) pieces of thin silver chain

Pair of silver ear wires

Fabric glue

TOOLS

2 flat-nose pliers

Round-nose pliers

Wire cutters

1. Attach a jump ring to a satin bow. Add a dab of fabric glue to secure the jump ring in place (Figure A).

2. String a heart bead onto a head pin. Make a loop in the head pin and trim any excess wire.

A

3. String a seed bead onto a head pin. Make a loop in the head pin and trim any excess wire. Repeat to string half of the seed beads onto head pins (Figure B).

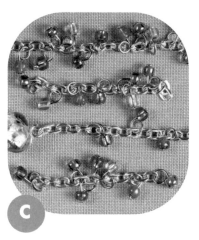

C

4. Cut one of the chains into 4 pieces, measuring the following lengths: 2½" (6.3 cm), 2¼" (5.7 cm), 1¾" (4.4 cm), and 1¼" (3.8 cm).

5. Attach the seed beads to the chains in a random fashion and attach the heart bead to the end of one of the chains. (Figure C).

6. Attach the chains to a jump ring (Figure D).

7. Attach the jump ring to the bow from Step 1.

8. Repeat Steps 1 to 7 to make the second earring. To finish, attach each bow to an ear wire.

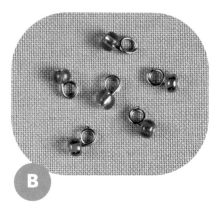

B

D

Golden Goddess Earrings

With delicate shell beads and elegant golden rings, these earrings evoke images of an ancient Greek goddess.

MATERIALS

38 square white flat shell beads, ¼" × ¼" (0.6 cm x 0.6 cm)

16 round white flat shell beads, ¼" (0.6 cm) in diameter

38 gold jump rings, ¼" (0.6 cm) in diameter

Pair of gold round drops, 1¼" (3 cm) in diameter

Pair of gold ear wires

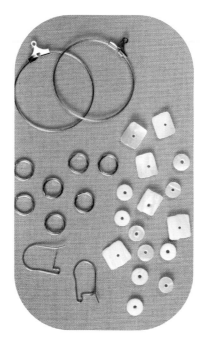

1. String a square bead onto a jump ring and close (Figure A).

2. String another square bead on another jump ring. Draw this jump ring through the jump ring from Step 1 and close (Figure B).

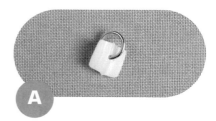

A

B

TOOLS

2 flat-nose pliers

Round-nose pliers

3. String another square bead onto another jump ring. Draw this jump ring through one of the jump rings in Step 2 and close. You should now have a chain of 3 jump rings, each of which has a square bead (Figure C).

4. Repeat the technique described in Steps 1 to 3 to make 5 chains. You'll need two 3-ring chains, two 4-ring chains, and one 5-ring chain (Figure D).

5. Open one of the drops and string a 3-ring chain, then 2 round beads (Figure E).

6. String a 4-ring chain, then 2 round beads (Figure F).

7. String a 5-ring chain, then 2 round beads (Figure G).

8. String a 4-ring chain, 2 round beads, and a 3-ring chain, then close the drop (Figure H).

9. Repeat Steps 1 to 8 to make the second earring. To finish, attach each earring to an ear wire.

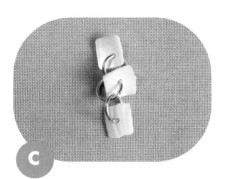

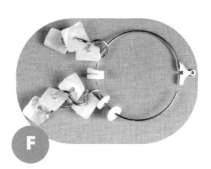

Swept Up in Snow Earrings

The translucent seed beads and delicate crystals in these earrings make them perfect for wintry weather.

MATERIALS

248 translucent white seed beads, size 11°

6 crystal bi-cone beads, ¼" (0.6 cm) in length

10 silver eye pins, 1" (2.5 cm) in length

10 silver head pins, 1" (2.5 cm) in length

14 silver jump rings, ⅛" (0.3 cm) in diameter

Pair of silver ear wires

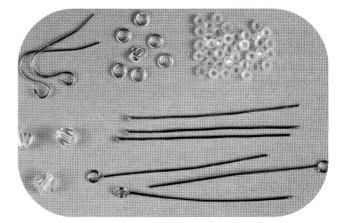

TOOLS

Round-nose pliers

Wire cutters

2 flat-nose pliers

1. String 15 seed beads onto an eye pin. Make a loop in the eye pin and trim any excess wire. Repeat to make another 15-bead eye pin.

2. String 11 seed beads onto an eye pin. Make a loop in the eye pin and trim any excess wire. Repeat to make another 11-bead eye pin.

3. String 14 seed beads onto a head pin. Make a loop in the head pin and trim any excess wire. Repeat to make another 14-bead head pin (Figure A).

4. String a crystal bead onto a head pin. String 10 seed beads, then make a loop in the head pin and trim any excess wire. Repeat to make another crystal-and-10-bead head pin.

5. String a crystal bead onto a head pin. String 14 seed beads, then make a loop in the head pin and trim any excess wire (Figure B).

6. String 1 seed bead onto an eye pin. String a crystal-and-10-bead eye pin from Step 4, then string 2 seed beads.

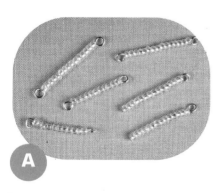

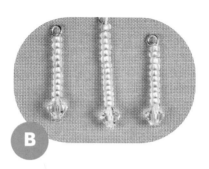

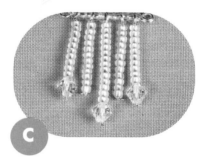

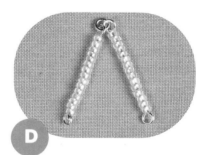

7. String a 14-bead head pin from Step 3, then string 2 seed beads. String the crystal-and-14-bead head pin from Step 5, then string 2 seed beads.

8. String the other 14-bead head pin from Step 3, then string 2 seed beads. String the other crystal-and-10-bead head pin from Step 4, then string 1 seed bead. Make a loop in the eye pin and trim any excess wire (Figure C).

9. Connect the 15-bead eye pins from Step 1 to each other with a jump ring (Figure D).

10. String a jump ring through the empty loop of one of the 15-bead eye pins. String an 11-bead eye pin from Step 2 onto the jump ring and close the jump ring. String another jump ring through the empty loop of the other 15-bead eye pin. String the other end of the 11-bead eye pin onto this jump ring and close the jump ring to form a triangle.

11. String jump rings onto both loops of the 11-bead eye pin you attached in Step 10 and use them to connect the other 11-bead eye pin (Figure E).

12. String jump rings onto the loops at either end of the bottommost 11-bead eye pin and attach the decorated eye pin from Step 8 (Figure F).

13. Repeat Steps 1 to 12 to make the second earring. To finish, attach each earring to an ear wire.

Rings & Brooches

Candy Shop Ring

This ring is as sweet as sweet can be. Make sure no one mistakes it for real candy!

MATERIALS

7 glass beads, various colors, ½" (1.3 cm) in diameter or smaller

7 silver eye pins

1 silver jump ring, ¼" (0.6 cm) in diameter

1 silver charm ring base

TOOLS

Round-nose pliers

Wire cutters

2 flat-nose pliers

1. String a bead onto an eye pin. Make a loop in the eye pin and trim any excess wire (Figure A).

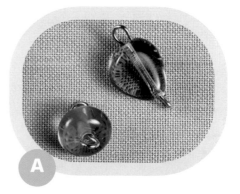

A

2. Repeat Step 1 to string all of the beads onto eye pins (Figure B).

3. String all of the eye pins onto the jump ring (Figure C).

4. Attach the jump ring to the loop in the ring base (Figure D).

C

B

D

Pink Peony Ring

Have a fresh flower on hand all the time with this beautiful bloom blossoming on your finger.

MATERIALS

300–400 seed beads, sizes 6°, 8°, 11°, various shades of orange, red, and pink

Memory wire for rings

Beading thread

TOOLS

Wire cutters

Round-nose pliers

Beading needle

1. Cut a 4-coil piece of memory wire and make a loop at one end using the round-nose pliers (Figure A).

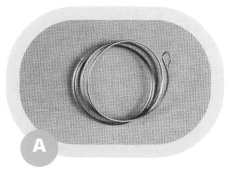

2. String beads onto the wire, alternating colors and sizes, until the coils are full. Make a loop at the other end to secure the beads in place (Figures B and C).

3. Thread the needle with a comfortable length of thread, fold the thread in half, and tie the ends together.

B

C

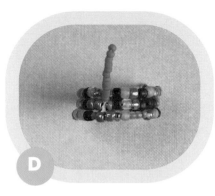

D

E

F

4. Tie the thread to one of the inner coils in the memory wire, near the center.

5. String 10–12 beads onto the thread. Loop the thread around the last bead and draw back through 9–12 beads to make a stick of beads. Draw the thread through one of the beads on the memory wire, preferably one that is size 6° or 8°, to secure in place (Figure D).

6. String 12–16 beads onto the thread and draw the thread back through the first bead to make a loop. Draw the thread through one of the beads on the memory wire to secure in place (Figure E).

7. Repeat Steps 5 and 6 until you have a lush flower in the middle of the ring (Figure F).

8. Tie the thread around the memory wire in a secure double knot and cut the thread close to the knot.

Very Victorian Brooch

The combination of delicate lace and silver gives this brooch an appearance that is both Victorian and modern. It's a striking blend that's sure to attract comments and compliments.

MATERIALS

7 round glass beads, various shades of pink and green

22 seed beads, size 8°, various shades of pink and green

4 oval shell beads

1 shell button, ¾" (1.9 cm) in diameter

31½" (80 cm) piece of thick silver chain

30" (76 cm) piece of lace ribbon, 2" (5 cm) wide

20" (51 cm) piece of lace ribbon, 1" (2.5 cm) wide

7 pairs of silver bead caps, sized to fit the glass beads

29 head pins

33 jump rings, ⅛" (0.3 cm) in diameter

Sewing thread

Pin back

TOOLS

Round-nose pliers

Scissors

Sewing needle

Wire cutters

2 flat-nose pliers

1. String a pair of bead caps and a glass bead onto a head pin, so that the bead caps cradle the glass bead. Make a loop in the head pin and trim any excess wire. Repeat to string all of the glass beads onto head pins (Figure A).

2. String a seed bead onto a head pin. Make a loop in the head pin and trim any excess wire. Repeat to string all of the seed beads onto head pins (Figure B).

3. Attach jump rings to all of the beads from Steps 1 and 2, and to all of the shell beads.

4. Cut the chain into 7 pieces, measuring the following lengths: 6" (15 cm), 5½" (14 cm), 5" (13 cm), 4½" (11 cm), 4" (10 cm), 3½" (9 cm), 3" (7.6 cm).

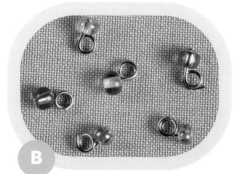

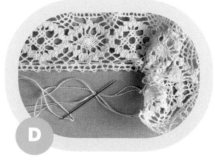

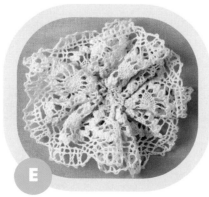

5. Attach the beads to the chains in a random fashion (Figure C).

6. Thread the needle with a comfortable length of thread, fold the thread in half, and tie the ends together.

7. Insert the thread at one end of the wide lace, near the edge. Make sure the thread is securely anchored and sew a wide running stitch to the other end.

8. Gently pull the thread to crinkle the lace into soft waves (Figure D).

9. Form a flower shape by pulling the thread gently and drawing the ends of the lace together. Sew the ends together securely with a couple of stitches (Figure E).

10. Sew the button on the front of the flower, in the middle (Figure F).

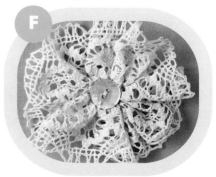

11. Sew the decorated chains and the pin back to the back of the flower (Figure G).

12. To finish, sew the thin lace ribbon to the back of the flower so that it hangs evenly from both sides, and covers the stitches securing the chains and pin back (Figure H).

Cool Kilt Brooch

I've chosen pink and sky blue accessories for this brooch, but you can choose any theme that expresses your unique sense of style.

MATERIALS

1 fabric bead, pink, ½" (1.3 cm) in diameter

8 special beads or pendants, various styles and shades

1 violet satin bow

1 pink silk tassel

1 silver chain tassel

4–8 eye pins

4–8 head pins

20 jump rings, ¼" (0.6 cm) in diameter

22" (56 cm) piece of silver chain

3-loop silver kilt pin

TOOLS

Round-nose pliers

Wire cutters

2 flat-nose pliers

1. String the fabric bead onto an eye pin. Make a loop in the eye pin and trim any excess wire. Repeat to string all of the beads onto either eye pins or head pins. Make a loop in each pin and trim any excess wire.

2. Attach jump rings to the beads and pendants (Figure A).

3. Attach jump rings to the bow and tassels (Figure B).

4. Attach the pink tassel to one of the special beads (Figure C).

C

A

D

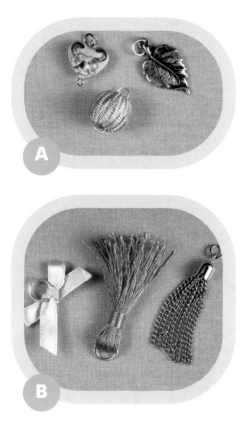

B

E

5. Cut the chain into 11 pieces, measuring the following lengths: 4" (10 cm), 3" (7.6 cm), 2¾" (7 cm), 2¼" (5.7 cm), 2" (5 cm), 1½" (3.8 cm), 1½" (3.8 cm), 1¼" (3 cm), 1¼" (3 cm), ¾" (1.9 cm), ¾" (1.9 cm).

6. Decorate 6 chains with the pendants and beads in a random fashion. Leave the other 5 chains plain (Figure D).

7. Attach 2 decorated chains and 2 plain chains to the fabric bead (Figure E).

8. Attach 2 decorated chains and 2 plain chains to the satin bow. Attach the bow to a loop on the kilt pin (Figure F).

9. Attach the fabric bead to a loop on the kilt pin (Figure G).

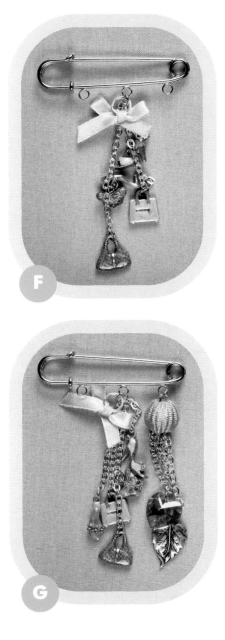

F

G

10. To finish, attach the
remaining chains to a jump
ring and attach to the third
loop on the kilt pin.

Index